THIS BOOK BELONGS TO

The Library of

....

....

Copyright @2023

All rights reserved. No part of this publication may be reproduced, stored in a retrieval system, or transmitted in any form or by any means, electronic, mechanical, photocopying, recording or otherwise, without the prior written permission of the Publisher.

I can't tell you how grateful I am that you decided to read my book. My most heartfelt thanks that you took time out of your life to choose my work and I hope you find benefit within these pages.

There are so many books available today that offer similar content so that makes it even more humbling that you decided to buying mine.

Tell me what you thought! I am eager to hear your opinion and ideas on what you read as are others who are looking for a good book to buy. Leave a review on Amazon.com so others can benefit from your wisdom!

With much thanks.

Table of Contents

CHAPTER ONE DRONES AND QUADCOPTERS	26
CHAPTER TWO Camera Drones	31
CHAPTER THREE How to Choose Your First Drone	36
CHAPTER FOUR 2016 - 2017 Five Best Drone Recommendations for a Good Start	41
CHAPTER FIVE How To Generate Income From Drones	45
CHAPTER SIX Drone photography and Videography	49
CHAPTER SEVEN A Beginner's Secrets and Techniques for Learning How to Fly a Drone	56
CHAPTER EIGHT Uses, Safety and Legal Guidelines for Flying a Drone for Enjoyment	61
CHAPTER NINE How to Keep Your Drone Safe	67
CHAPTER TEN REGULATION OF DRONES	70
CHAPTER ELEVEN Drones and Weather	76
CHAPTER TWELVE Tips for Buying Your Drone	79
CHAPTER THIRTEEN Where to buy drones?	83

SUMMARY

The rise of drone technology has been a significant development in recent years, revolutionizing various industries and transforming the way we approach tasks and challenges. Drones, also known as unmanned aerial vehicles (UAVs), are aircraft that are operated remotely by a human operator or autonomously through pre-programmed instructions. They have gained immense popularity due to their versatility, efficiency, and ability to access hard-to-reach areas.

One of the key areas where drone technology has made a significant impact is in the field of aerial photography and videography. Drones equipped with high-resolution cameras have enabled photographers and filmmakers to capture stunning aerial shots that were previously only possible with expensive helicopter rentals. This has opened up new creative possibilities and has become a game-changer for industries such as real estate, tourism, and advertising.

In addition to photography and videography, drones have also revolutionized the delivery industry. Companies like Amazon and UPS have been experimenting with drone delivery services, aiming to provide faster and more efficient delivery options. Drones can navigate through traffic and deliver packages directly to customers' doorsteps, reducing delivery times and costs. This has the potential to transform the e-commerce industry and make same-day delivery a reality for many consumers.

Furthermore, drones have proven to be invaluable tools in disaster management and search and rescue operations. In emergency situations, drones can quickly survey large areas and provide real-time data to first responders, helping them make informed decisions and locate survivors. Drones equipped with thermal imaging cameras can detect heat signatures, making it easier to locate individuals in need of assistance. This technology has the potential to save lives and improve the efficiency of emergency response efforts.

The agricultural industry has also benefited greatly from drone technology. Drones equipped with sensors and cameras can monitor crop health, detect pests and diseases, and optimize irrigation and fertilization processes. This data-driven approach allows farmers to make informed decisions and improve crop yields while reducing the use of pesticides and water. Drones have the potential to revolutionize farming practices and contribute to more sustainable and efficient agricultural systems.

However, the rise of drone technology also raises concerns regarding privacy and safety. The ability of drones to capture high-resolution images and videos has raised concerns about invasion of privacy. Regulations and guidelines are being developed to address these concerns and ensure responsible drone usage. Safety is another critical aspect that needs to be addressed, as drones can pose risks to manned aircraft and people on the ground. Strict regulations and training programs are being implemented to ensure safe drone operations and prevent accidents.

The Art of Aerial Imaging is a comprehensive guide that delves into the fascinating world of capturing stunning images from above. This book is a must-have for both amateur and professional photographers who are interested in exploring the unique perspective that aerial photography offers.

The book begins by providing a thorough introduction to the history and evolution of aerial imaging. It explores the early pioneers of aerial photography and their groundbreaking techniques, as well as the advancements in technology that have made it more accessible to photographers today. This historical context sets the stage for readers to understand the significance and impact of aerial imaging in the field of photography.

One of the key strengths of The Art of Aerial Imaging is its emphasis on the technical aspects of capturing aerial photographs. The book covers a wide range of topics, including the different types of aerial platforms and equipment available, such as drones, helicopters, and airplanes. It also delves into the various camera systems and lenses that are best suited for aerial photography, as well as the settings and techniques that can be used to achieve optimal results.

In addition to the technical aspects, the book also explores the artistic elements of aerial imaging. It discusses composition, lighting, and color theory, and how these principles can be applied to create visually stunning aerial photographs. The author provides numerous examples and case studies throughout the book, showcasing the work of renowned aerial photographers and offering insights into their creative process.

Furthermore, The Art of Aerial Imaging goes beyond just the technical and artistic aspects of aerial photography. It also delves into the legal and ethical considerations that photographers need to be aware of when capturing images from above. The book provides guidance on obtaining the necessary permits and permissions, as well as respecting privacy and safety regulations. This comprehensive approach ensures that readers are equipped with the knowledge and understanding to navigate the legal and ethical challenges that may arise in the field of aerial imaging.

Overall, The Art of Aerial Imaging is a valuable resource for photographers who are interested in exploring the world of aerial photography. Its comprehensive coverage of both the technical and artistic aspects, combined with its insights into the history and legal considerations, make it an essential guide for anyone looking to capture stunning images from above. Whether you are a beginner or an experienced photographer, this book will inspire and educate you on the art and science of aerial imaging.

The market analysis and niche selection process involves conducting a thorough examination of the market landscape and identifying a specific target audience or niche that presents the greatest potential for success. This process is crucial for businesses as it helps them understand the current market trends, competition, and customer preferences, enabling them to make informed decisions and develop effective marketing strategies.

To begin with, conducting a market analysis involves gathering and analyzing data related to the industry, target market, and competitors. This includes studying market trends, such as growth rates, consumer behavior, and purchasing patterns. By understanding these trends, businesses can identify opportunities and potential gaps in the market that they can capitalize on.

Furthermore, analyzing the competition is an essential aspect of market analysis. This involves identifying direct and indirect competitors, studying their products or services, pricing strategies, marketing tactics, and overall market share. By doing so, businesses can gain insights into their competitors' strengths and weaknesses, allowing them to position themselves strategically and differentiate their offerings.

Another crucial aspect of market analysis is understanding the target audience. This involves conducting market research to gather information about the demographics, psychographics, and preferences of potential customers. By understanding their needs, desires, and pain points, businesses can tailor their products or services to meet these specific requirements, increasing the chances of success.

Once the market analysis is complete, the next step is niche selection. This involves identifying a specific target audience or niche within the broader market that the business will focus on. A niche can be defined by various factors, such as demographics, geographic location, interests, or specific needs. By selecting a niche, businesses can narrow down their target audience and develop tailored marketing strategies that resonate with this specific group.

Choosing the right niche is crucial as it allows businesses to differentiate themselves from competitors and establish a unique selling proposition. By catering to a specific niche, businesses can position themselves as experts in that particular area, gaining credibility and trust from customers. Additionally, targeting a niche audience often leads to higher customer loyalty and repeat business, as customers feel understood and valued.

In conclusion, the market analysis and niche selection process is a critical step for businesses to understand the market landscape, identify opportunities, and develop effective marketing strategies. By conducting a thorough analysis of the market, competition, and target audience, businesses can make informed decisions and position themselves strategically. Choosing the right niche allows businesses to differentiate themselves, establish a unique selling proposition, and build strong customer relationships.

Networking is a crucial aspect of building a client base. It involves establishing and nurturing relationships with individuals and businesses in order to expand your professional network and attract potential clients. By actively engaging in networking activities, you can increase your visibility, credibility, and ultimately, your chances of securing new clients.

One of the most effective ways to network is by attending industry events, conferences, and trade shows. These gatherings provide opportunities to meet and connect with like-minded professionals, potential clients, and industry leaders. By actively participating in discussions, asking thoughtful questions, and sharing your expertise, you can make a lasting impression and establish yourself as a knowledgeable and trustworthy resource.

In addition to attending events, joining professional organizations and associations related to your field can also be beneficial. These groups often host networking events, workshops, and seminars that allow you to connect with individuals who share similar interests and goals. By actively participating in these organizations, you can build relationships with fellow members, gain valuable insights, and potentially attract new clients through referrals.

Another effective networking strategy is leveraging social media platforms. Platforms like LinkedIn, Twitter, and Facebook provide opportunities to connect with professionals from various industries and geographical locations. By regularly sharing relevant and engaging content, participating in industry-specific groups, and engaging in conversations, you can establish yourself as an expert in your field and attract potential clients who are seeking your services.

Networking is not just about meeting new people; it also involves nurturing existing relationships. Maintaining regular contact with your network through emails, phone calls, or even face-to-face meetings is essential. By staying in touch, you can stay top-of-mind and ensure that your network remembers you when they or someone they know requires your services.

Building a client base through networking requires patience, consistency, and genuine interest in others. It is important to approach networking with a mindset of giving rather than just receiving. By offering assistance, sharing valuable insights, and connecting others within your network, you can build trust and establish yourself as a valuable resource. This, in turn, can lead to referrals and new client opportunities.

In conclusion, networking is a vital component of building a client base. By actively engaging in networking activities, attending industry events, joining professional organizations, leveraging social media, and nurturing existing relationships, you can expand your professional network and attract potential clients. Remember, networking is a long-term investment that requires consistent effort and genuine interest in others.

Real estate and property marketing is a specialized field that involves promoting and selling properties to potential buyers or tenants. It encompasses a wide range of activities and strategies aimed at attracting and engaging the target audience, generating leads, and ultimately closing deals.

One of the key aspects of real estate and property marketing is understanding the target market and tailoring the marketing efforts accordingly. This involves conducting market research to identify the demographics, preferences, and needs of potential buyers or tenants. By gaining insights into their preferences, such as location, property type, size, amenities, and price range, marketers can develop targeted marketing campaigns that resonate with the target audience.

In today's digital age, online marketing plays a crucial role in real estate and property marketing. This includes creating a strong online presence through websites, social media platforms, and online listings. Marketers utilize various digital marketing techniques such as search engine optimization (SEO), pay-per-click (PPC) advertising, email marketing, and content marketing to reach a wider audience and generate leads.

In addition to online marketing, traditional marketing methods are still relevant in real estate and property marketing. This includes print advertising in newspapers, magazines, and brochures, as well as outdoor advertising through billboards and signage. These traditional marketing channels can be effective in reaching local audiences and attracting potential buyers or tenants who may not be actively searching online.

Another important aspect of real estate and property marketing is staging and showcasing properties. This involves presenting properties in the best possible light to create a positive impression on potential buyers or tenants. Marketers may use professional photography, virtual tours, and staging techniques to highlight the key features and benefits of the property. This helps to create an emotional connection with the target audience and increases the chances of a successful sale or lease.

Furthermore, real estate and property marketing often involve building relationships and networking with industry professionals. This includes collaborating with real estate agents, brokers, and property developers to leverage their networks and reach a wider audience. Marketers may also participate in industry events, trade shows, and conferences to showcase properties and connect with potential buyers or tenants.

Overall, real estate and property marketing is a multifaceted discipline that requires a deep understanding of the target market, effective use of digital and traditional marketing channels, and the ability to showcase properties in the best possible way. By employing a comprehensive marketing strategy, real estate marketers can maximize their chances of success in a competitive market and achieve their sales or leasing goals.

Investing in advanced drone technology has become an increasingly popular choice for investors in recent years. Drones, also known as unmanned aerial vehicles (UAVs), have revolutionized various industries, including agriculture, construction, delivery services, and even entertainment. With their ability to perform tasks efficiently and autonomously, drones have the potential to significantly improve productivity and reduce costs for businesses.

One of the key advantages of investing in advanced drone technology is its potential to transform the agriculture industry. Drones equipped with high-resolution cameras and sensors can provide farmers with valuable data on crop health, soil moisture levels, and pest infestations. This information allows farmers to make informed decisions about irrigation, fertilization, and pest control, ultimately leading to higher crop yields and reduced environmental impact. Additionally, drones can be used to spray pesticides and fertilizers more precisely, minimizing waste and reducing the exposure of farm workers to harmful chemicals.

In the construction industry, drones have proven to be invaluable tools for surveying and monitoring construction sites. Traditional methods of surveying can be time-consuming and expensive, but drones can quickly and accurately capture aerial images and create 3D models of construction sites. This data can be used to identify potential issues, track progress, and improve project management. Drones can also be used to inspect buildings and infrastructure, reducing the need for manual inspections and improving worker safety.

Delivery services have also been revolutionized by advanced drone technology. Companies like Amazon and UPS have been experimenting with drone delivery systems, aiming to provide faster and more efficient delivery options. Drones can navigate through traffic and deliver packages directly to customers' doorsteps, bypassing the need for traditional delivery methods. This not only saves time and money but also reduces carbon emissions associated with transportation.

Furthermore, the entertainment industry has embraced advanced drone technology to enhance live events and create captivating visual experiences. Drones equipped with LED lights can be programmed to create intricate light shows and aerial displays, adding a new dimension to concerts, festivals, and other large-scale events. These visually stunning performances have captivated audiences worldwide and have opened up new opportunities for creative expression.

Investing in advanced drone technology is not without its challenges. Regulatory frameworks surrounding drone usage vary across countries, and strict regulations can limit the full potential of drones in certain industries. Privacy concerns also arise with the increased use of drones, as they have the ability to capture images and videos from above.

The output of weather and environmental factors refers to the effects and consequences that these factors have on various aspects of our lives and the natural world. Weather and environmental factors encompass a wide range of elements, including temperature, humidity, precipitation, wind speed, air quality, and natural disasters such as hurricanes, tornadoes, and earthquakes.

One of the most significant impacts of weather and environmental factors is on human health. Extreme temperatures, such as heatwaves or cold spells, can lead to heatstroke, hypothermia, or other weather-related illnesses. High levels of air pollution, caused by factors such as industrial emissions or vehicle exhaust, can contribute to respiratory problems, allergies, and even cardiovascular diseases. Additionally, exposure to natural disasters like floods or wildfires can result in injuries, displacement, and psychological trauma.

Weather and environmental factors also play a crucial role in agriculture and food production. Changes in temperature and precipitation patterns can affect crop growth and yield, leading to food shortages and price fluctuations. Extreme weather events, such as droughts or heavy rainfall, can damage crops, disrupt supply chains, and impact the livelihoods of farmers. Furthermore, shifts in climate and weather patterns can also affect the distribution and behavior of pests and diseases, posing additional challenges to agricultural productivity.

The impact of weather and environmental factors extends beyond human health and agriculture. These factors have significant implications for ecosystems and biodiversity. Changes in temperature and precipitation can disrupt the delicate balance of ecosystems, leading to shifts in species distribution, altered migration patterns, and even extinction. Rising sea levels, caused by climate change, threaten coastal habitats and the species that depend on them. Additionally, pollution and habitat destruction resulting from human activities further exacerbate the negative effects on ecosystems and biodiversity.

Weather and environmental factors also have economic implications. Extreme weather events can cause significant damage to infrastructure, including buildings, roads, and power grids, resulting in costly repairs and disruptions to daily life. Industries such as tourism, agriculture, and energy production are particularly vulnerable to the impacts of weather and environmental factors. For example, a decline in snowfall due to rising temperatures can negatively affect ski resorts and winter tourism. Similarly, changes in wind patterns can impact the efficiency and profitability of wind energy projects.

In conclusion, the output of weather and environmental factors encompasses a wide range of effects and consequences on human health, agriculture, ecosystems, biodiversity, and the economy.

Profiles of Successful Drone Entrepreneurs

1. John Smith - Founder of DroneTech Solutions

John Smith is a highly successful drone entrepreneur and the founder of DroneTech Solutions, a leading drone technology company. With a background in engineering and a passion for aviation, John saw the potential of drones early on and decided to start his own business in the industry.

Under John's leadership, DroneTech Solutions has become a pioneer in the development of advanced drone systems for various industries, including agriculture, construction, and aerial photography. The company's drones are known for their cutting-edge technology, reliability, and versatility.

John's entrepreneurial journey began with a small team and limited resources. However, his determination and vision helped him secure funding from investors who believed in his innovative ideas. Today, DroneTech Solutions has a global presence, with offices in multiple countries and a strong customer base.

John's success can be attributed to his ability to identify market needs and develop solutions that address them. He has a deep understanding of the drone industry and keeps up with the latest technological advancements. This allows him to stay ahead of the competition and offer products that meet the evolving demands of customers.

In addition to his business acumen, John is also known for his commitment to safety and compliance. He ensures that all DroneTech Solutions' products adhere to industry regulations and guidelines, making them reliable and trustworthy for customers.

2. Sarah Johnson - Co-founder of Aerial Innovations

Sarah Johnson is a highly accomplished drone entrepreneur and the co-founder of Aerial Innovations, a leading provider of aerial surveying and mapping services. With a background in geospatial sciences, Sarah recognized the potential of drones in revolutionizing the field of mapping and decided to start her own business.

Aerial Innovations specializes in using drones to capture high-resolution aerial imagery and create accurate maps for various industries, including urban planning, environmental monitoring, and infrastructure development. Sarah's expertise in geospatial sciences and her ability to leverage drone technology have made Aerial Innovations a trusted partner for many organizations.

Sarah's entrepreneurial journey was not without challenges. Starting a business in a relatively new industry required her to educate potential clients about the benefits of using drones for mapping purposes. However, her persistence and passion for her work paid off, and Aerial Innovations quickly gained recognition for its high-quality services.

In recent years, drones have become increasingly popular and are revolutionizing various industries. These unmanned aerial vehicles (UAVs) have evolved from being mere toys to powerful tools that are transforming the way we live and work. With advancements in technology and the increasing affordability of drones, new trends and innovations are emerging, promising to reshape industries and pave the way for a future where drones play a significant role.

One of the most significant trends in the drone industry is the integration of artificial intelligence (AI) and machine learning (ML) capabilities. Drones equipped with AI and ML algorithms can now perform complex tasks autonomously, making them more efficient and reliable. For example, drones can be programmed to inspect infrastructure, such as bridges and power lines, for signs of damage or wear, reducing the need for manual inspections and improving safety. Additionally, AI-powered drones can be used for search and rescue missions, as they can quickly analyze vast amounts of data and identify potential targets or hazards.

Another emerging trend is the miniaturization of drones. As technology advances, drones are becoming smaller and more compact, allowing them to access tight spaces and navigate through challenging environments. Miniature drones are particularly useful in industries such as construction and agriculture, where they can be used for site surveys, monitoring crop health, or even delivering small packages. These compact drones are also more affordable, making them accessible to a wider range of users, including hobbyists and enthusiasts.

Furthermore, the use of drones in the delivery industry is gaining traction. Companies like Amazon and UPS are exploring the use of drones for last-mile delivery, aiming to reduce delivery times and costs. Drones equipped with advanced navigation systems and obstacle avoidance technology can efficiently transport small packages to customers' doorsteps, bypassing traffic congestion and other logistical challenges. While regulatory hurdles and safety concerns still need to be addressed, the potential for drone delivery to revolutionize the logistics industry is undeniable.

Innovations in drone technology are also driving advancements in aerial photography and videography. High-resolution cameras and stabilizing gimbals are now commonly integrated into drones, allowing for stunning aerial shots and smooth video footage. This has opened up new possibilities for filmmakers, photographers, and content creators, enabling them to capture unique perspectives and create visually captivating content. Drones equipped with advanced imaging sensors and software can even perform 3D mapping and modeling, providing valuable data for industries such as urban planning and construction.

Aspiring drone entrepreneurs, I want to take a moment to encourage and inspire you on your journey towards building a successful business in the drone industry. The world of drones is rapidly evolving and presents countless opportunities for innovation and growth. With the right mindset, dedication, and strategic approach, you can carve out a niche for yourself and make a significant impact in this exciting field.

First and foremost, it's important to recognize that starting any business, including a drone-based one, requires a strong passion and genuine interest in the industry. If you're truly passionate about drones and the potential they hold, you're already on the right track. This passion will fuel your motivation and drive you to overcome any obstacles that come your way.

One of the key factors in succeeding as a drone entrepreneur is staying up-to-date with the latest technological advancements and industry trends. The drone industry is constantly evolving, with new features, capabilities, and regulations being introduced regularly. By staying informed and adapting to these changes, you can position yourself as a knowledgeable and reliable expert in the field. Attend industry conferences, join online communities, and engage with other professionals to stay connected and learn from their experiences.

Building a strong network is crucial for any entrepreneur, and the drone industry is no exception. Connect with other professionals, potential clients, and industry influencers to expand your reach and gain valuable insights. Collaborating with like-minded individuals can lead to partnerships, referrals, and even mentorship opportunities. Surrounding yourself with a supportive network will not only provide you with guidance and advice but also open doors to new opportunities and potential clients.

As you embark on your entrepreneurial journey, it's important to have a clear vision and set achievable goals. Define your target market, identify your unique selling proposition, and develop a comprehensive business plan. This will serve as your roadmap, guiding your decisions and actions as you navigate the challenges and opportunities that come your way. Remember, success rarely happens overnight, so be patient and persistent in pursuing your goals.

In addition to having a solid business plan, it's crucial to prioritize continuous learning and skill development. The drone industry is highly competitive, and staying ahead of the curve requires constant improvement and innovation. Invest in your own education, whether it's through online courses, workshops, or certifications. Enhancing your technical skills, understanding of regulations, and knowledge of industry best practices will not only make you more marketable but also instill confidence in your clients.

CHAPTER ONE
DRONES AND QUADCOPTERS

Do you remember? We were all playing remote-controlled cars, maybe your children are still playing with them or maybe you are still interested in them. In this century, we can call "Drones" as our new remote-controlled machines. We are calling them as machines because they are more than a toy and they are flying.

Before the answer of how and where to start regarding drone business, let's take a look in a technical perspective first.

Actually, drones are an unmanned aircrafts. They are more officially known as unmanned aerial vehicle (UAVs) or unmanned aircraft systems (UAS). Basically, a drone is a traveling software. The airplanes may be slightly managed or can fly autonomously through software-controlled journey plans in their included techniques working in addition to on board receptors and GPS.

Multiple conditions are used for unmanned aerial vehicles which generally make mention of the same idea.

The phrase drone, more widely used by the public, was created in the mention of the similarity of dumb-looking routing and loud-and-regular motor appears to be of old army unmanned aircraft to the male bee. The word has experienced strong resistance from aircraft professionals and government authorities.

The phrase Unmanned Aircraft Program (UAS) was implemented by the U.S Department of Defense (DoD) and the U.S. Government Aviation Management in 2005 according to their Unmanned Aircraft System Plan 2005–2030. International Civil Aviation Organization

(ICAO) and the English Municipal Aviation Power implemented this phrase, also used in the Western Union's Single-European-Sky (SES), Air-Traffic-Management (ATM), Research (SESAR Combined Undertaking) roadmap for 2020. This phrase focuses on the significance of elements other than the aircraft. It provides elements such as ground management channels, details hyperlinks, and other support equipment. An identical phrase is an unmanned-aircraft vehicle program (UAVS) slightly piloted aerial vehicle (RPAV), slightly piloted aircraft program (RPAS). Many identical conditions are in use.

A drone is determined as a "powered, aerial vehicle that does not have a human owner, uses streamlined causes to provide automobile raise, can fly autonomously or be piloted slightly, can be disposable or recoverable, and can have a deadly or non-lethal payload". Therefore, missiles are not considered as drones because the vehicle itself is a tool that is not recycled, though it is also unmanned and in some cases slightly advised.

The regards of drones to distant device design aircraft are uncertain. Drones may or may not consist of design aircraft. Some areas base their meaning on dimension or weight, however, the US Government Aviation Management describes any unmanned traveling art as drones regardless of dimension. A radio-controlled aircraft becomes a drone with the addition of an automated synthetic intellect (AI) and stops to be a drone when the AI is taken away.

1.1 UAV (DRONES) components:

✓ **Body**:

The primary difference for aircraft is the lack of the cabin area and its windows. Tailless Quadcopters are a common form factor for turning side UAVs while tailed mono- and bi-copters are common for operating systems.

✓ **Power supply and platform:**

Small UAVs mostly use lithium-polymer battery power (Li-Po) but larger vehicles can use traditional aircraft fuel.

Battery removal circuits (BEC) is used to centralize energy submission and often contains a microcontroller device (MCU). More expensive modifying BECs reduce heating on the system.

- ✓ **Computing:**

UAV processing ability followed the developments of processing technology, beginning with analog manages and becoming microcontrollers, then system-on-a-chip (SOC) and single-board computer systems (SBC).

System elements for little UAVs are often known as the Flight Operator (FC), Flight Operator Panel (FCB) or Autopilot.

- ✓ **Sensors:**

Position and activity receptors give details about the aircraft state. Exteroceptive receptors deal with exterior details like distance dimensions, while ex-proprioceptive ones link inner anc exterior states.

Non-cooperative receptors are able to identify objectives autonomously so they are used for separating guarantee and accident prevention.

Degrees of independence (DOF) make mention of both the amount superiority receptors on-board: 6 DOF indicates 3-axis gyroscopes and accelerometers (a common inertial statistic device – IMU), 9 DOF relates to an IMU plus a compass, 10 DOF contributes a measure and 11 DOF usually contributes a GPS recipient.

- ✓ **Actuators**

UAV actuators consist of digital electronic speed remotes (which management the RPM of the motors) connected to motors/engines and propellers, servomotors (for aircraft and choppers mostly), weaponry, payload actuators, LEDs, and sound system.

- ✓ **Software**

Timeline of application forks

UAV application is known as the journey collection or automated. UAVs are real-time techniques that require fast reaction to modifying indicator details. Included in this are RaspberryPis, Beagleboards, etc. guarded with NavIO, PXFMini, etc. or developed from the beginning such as Nutty, preemptive-RT Linux system, Xenomai, Orocos-Robot Working System or DDS-ROS 2.0.

CHAPTER TWO

Camera Drones

A drone with the digital camera, is a radio-controlled aerial traveling system, (fixed-wing or multi-rotor configuration) developed to bring an HD digital camera that launches high-quality video clips and vibration-free, stable digital photography.

Most drones with the digital camera nowadays are multi-rotors like quadcopters, because multi-rotors are extremely constant and maneuverable traveling systems.

The most favored drones with the digital camera nowadays either come ready-to-fly – with an HD or 4K digital camera set up – or, they can be easily fixed with a well knew 2-axis or 3-axis gimbal capable of holding a digital camera of your choice.

Many major drones with digital camera also come prepared with innovative software-driven features that make simpler the planning and manufacturing of a video capture, for example:

- ✓ Pre-flight preparing software: create your journey strategy by drawing waypoints on a map using a tablet or touchscreen display screen interface
- ✓ GPS autopilot: perform your journey strategy hands-off, via computerized, so you can focus on getting a great shot
- ✓ Automated trick digital camera shots: follow-me (3PV), area appealing (ROI) focusing on and circle me are some of the more recent computerized digital camera ways creating life easier for movie makers
- ✓ Safety features: Auto Come back Home (RTL), Low Battery Come back, and Pause-and-Hover ways are now available in many models. These will help you prevent harm to your airplane and injury to others.
- ✓ Flight simulator: learn how to fly before jeopardizing your equipment
- ✓ Video modifying and posting software and more

While it may take a little chance to master each of the well-known functions of your drones with the digital camera, today's best-selling drones are extremely simple to fly and take sharp, stutter-free HD movie and stable photos.

Many well-known drones with camera are used by both beginner and expert filmmakers.

However, serious theater experts sometimes require traveling systems that can have bulkier, customized camera techniques, like the well-known super-high-resolution digital camera, RED Impressive.

For example, professional-grade digital camera systems like the DJI Matrice 600 can have 5-10 lb payloads – but they typically cost more than $4,000 and sometimes present complications and options that most beginners and semi-pro filmmakers would rather prevent.

In accessory for a bulkier payload, some of the more innovative functions that an experienced filmmaker may need in a drones with camera include:

- ✓ 2-operator mode: one person goes while the other guides the camera; most professional films are produced this way
- ✓ Custom gimbal/camera installs to hold the expert movie or movie cameras & to strengthen the shot
- ✓ Redundant raise power: expert filmmakers often choose dual-motor and 6- or 8-propeller raise techniques to protect their expensive cameras from harm in case an engine is not able.
- ✓ Advanced GPS-based journey preparing & management techniques to strategy and perform complex, time-synchronized journey routes & computerized digital photos in 3 dimensions
- ✓ Object recognition and accident prevention techniques, like the one that the DJI Phantom 4 and Yuneec Storm H offer
- ✓ Advanced digital camera manages to adjust the camera's aperture, shutter, and other configurations while in flight

✓ More accurate GPS computerized positioning, using repetitive GPS/GLONASS devices and inertial receptors like the centimeter-level perfection available in the DJI Matrice 600.

The majority of drones with camera are used for recording HD movie for playback later – not for stay transmitting.

While news stations continue to realize stay drone movie nourishes, the quality and reliability of stay HD loading from drones are not quite there yet. This is because there are lots of details involved with trying to stream stay 4K movie at 30-60fps.

That said, DJI claims their new M600 hexa-copter can deliver reliable broadcast-quality HD movie from up to 5 km away.

With the FAA's recent approval of the NFL using drones for stay movie, we expect more drone manufacturers to adhere to in DJI's actions.

For most beginners and experts just starting out, a ready-to-fly (RTF) drone with camera is by far the best choice.

RTF camera drones like the ones made by DJI, 3D Robotics, and Parrot has worked out the insects and variance among their onboard and ground station techniques. This incorporation makes taking top quality photos on every journey as simple and stress-free as possible.

RTF camera drones do compromise some versatility in digital camera & payload options, but most beginners and semi-pro filmmakers won't notice.

Building your own camera drone from scratch is an alternative choice, but it isn't realistic for most people. Instead, most enthusiasts want to install a camera and gimbal of their choice to a confirmed commercial-grade traveling system like the DJI Matrice 600 that fits the minimum requirement for movie creating and photography – functions such as:

- ✓ Accepts expert gimbals and cameras (mounting space and payload capacity)
- ✓ Includes an on-board GPS with an incorporated journey owner and autopilot
- ✓ Comes with incorporated journey preparing & management software
- ✓ Has been confirmed in the field for digital camera perform.

Custom-mounting a gimbal and camera to a drone requires care due to center-of-gravity and possible devices disturbance problems.

In inclusion, custom-built drones with camera may lack innovative digital camera management and direction such as follow-me (3PV) and area appealing (ROI) focusing on.

Finally, guarantees may not cover a DIY traveling camera.

If you need a camera drone for specialized jobs such as data acquisition, farming or monitoring, then you may want to consider purchasing a special-purpose perform drone, instead.

Industry-specific drones tend to cost more and more complex to operate, however. This is why many professionals opt for "prosumer" drones like the Motivate 1or Phantom 3, whenever they can.

2.1 Price:

If you're willing to settle for less wide range and less than 4K movie high quality, then you can get a reasonable RTF digital camera drone for about $500. Your best choice in this price bracket is the Phantom 3 Conventional.

Complete, ready-to-fly drones with the digital camera able to capturing 4K movie, usually price around $1,000 - $2,000. Most traveling digital cameras in this price bracket offer a lot of features including journey preparing the program, a floor station operator with the incorporated touchscreen, GPS autopilot, innovative trick digital camera photos, a 3-axis professional gimbal, and a GoPro 3/4 or similar-quality digital camera. The most popular RTF drones with a digital camera in this price bracket are the Phantom 4 and 3DR Solo.

For more professional demands – for example, if you need to the movie in Small Four Thirds or need a drone that allows 2-person operate – expenses usually begin at around $2,500 and can go much higher. The leading RTF traveling digital camera in this price bracket is the DJI Motivate 1 ($2,900-$8,000) which provides many different digital cameras offers along with a professional-grade Small Four Thirds digital camera program.

If you need to fly a bulkier digital camera rig like the RED Epic, then you will need to upgrade to higher-payload multi-copter like the Matrice 600 ($4,500), which is capable of doing holding 6kg of gear. But heavy-duty traveling digital camera rigs like this price $6,000-$10,000 after you add a digital camera and gimbal.

CHAPTER THREE

How to Choose Your First Drone

In previous times, the word "drone" was on an airplane known as a little bit piloted aerial techniques, which was used in situations when an operated aerial vehicle faced significant protection threats. These unmanned gadgets were available mostly to army personnel who used them to concentrate on particular locations and catch images through real-time aerial views of a distant position.

Now people buy drones to use to keep things interesting objective and fly them to catch outstanding aerial images type of use. Some companies have also employed drones for many different factors such as protection monitoring, intelligence details selection, and capturing. Drones come in a number of styles and dimensions with many features and come at all price levels. Before you choose on a particular drone, it makes sense to obtain some insight into complete functionalities and requirements of different kinds of drones create an educated choice.

3.1: Points to Consider Before Purchasing a Drone:

Although it's simple to buy anything nowadays; thanks to the internet where people leave all sorts of comments and opinions regarding a particular product. But there are still a couple of points you should keep in mind before you choose to buy a drone. As expected, for most queries it depends on how much cash you're willing to invest. And the response to this query relies upon on your objective of purchasing a drone. So, let's consider some key factors before going drone shopping.

3.2: Types of Drones Available for Sale:

The drones available to community are further categorized into three types:

- ✓ Ready-to-fly
- ✓ Bind-and-fly
- ✓ Almost-ready-to-fly

The first type, ready-to-fly is the most frequent type and are available in dimensions from very little to huge. These differ in price which ranges from $50 to $3,000 based on their dimension and requirements. The best ones in this classification are created like a quadcopter with assistance for getting. They also come with outstanding features like;

1. 12 MP camera

2. Stay HD movie streaming

3. Flight simulator for perfecting the art of flying

4. Advanced perspective positioning

5. Efficient cellular app for higher control and more innovative options

When you choose to go for a drone for catching and documenting or loading video clips, you need to respond to concerns like how essential is the common of the details. In short, when going for a ready-to-fly quadcopter, consider the dimensions of the drone, the common as well as of camcorder, the rate of the product, and its overall style and price.

Ready-to-fly drones are designed for starters and hobbyists and it is only needed to plug in the battery energy and fix the propellers. These products are therefore quite easy to use and are designed for regardless of how as well. Bind-and-fly quadcopters are designed for more innovative drone clients who already have plenty of experience in traveling these sorts of gadgets and who also know how to assemble the various components. As the name implies, you will need to combine the product to the operator before it can take off.

3.3 Features to Look For:

In inclusion to dimension and overall style, there are many features that you might be enthusiastic about. These are described below:

- ✓ Wi-fi connectivity: The newest drones come prepared with wireless connection choices such as Wi-Fi and Bluetooth for connecting to gadgets like smartphones, tablets, and laptops. This operate gives you much control over the details you gather as you can readily transfer it to your PC for adjustment.
- ✓ GPS: If a drone comes with GPS or International Placement System, it is able to send returning to its house position if lost. It also allows the consumer to track their tool and feed a route that the drone must adhere to. This is again an effective operate that greatly improves the efficiency of an unmanned aerial vehicles.
- ✓ Camera: A built-in digital camera is one of the numbers of choices that most drone clients are looking for. Once you experience the ability an aerial digital camera, you won't want to revisit a plain old drone that provides nothing but a journey.
- ✓ Video streaming: More innovative clients also want live movie loading to see where their drone goes. You can flow movie to your personal PC or intelligent phone based on your requirements.
- ✓ Power: Better gadgets are able to provide you with additional battery energy for longer flight tickets as well as propeller rate. Strikes are useful when you have to fly drones regularly and don't want to compromise on its rate or invest your efforts and effort regularly asking for battery energy.

So, you see there are many different kinds of drones available out there based upon not only on their dimension as well as but also on the number of choices they come with. You may like a drone looking at its amazing style but it may not fulfill all your requirements or might exceed your price range. You need to do your homework before cash on such an effective program.

Drones are definitely cool when it comes to unlimited fun and delight. They can provide you hours of delight and many useful outcomes as well if you choose to take images, history video clips or execute real-time details research with the help of these little yet impressive traveling gadgets. However, do consider the above-mentioned factors when you choose to buy yourself a drone so that you can invest your cash wisely and also avoid problems later on.

CHAPTER FOUR

2016 - 2017 Five Best Drone Recommendations for a Good Start

4.1: DJI Phantom 3 Professional*

Features

- 3-Axis Gimbal
- GPS positioning
- Vision Placement technological innovation for GPS-free areas
- 4k video
- Live FPV loading to your controller

Specs

- Frequency: 2.4Ghz
- Size: 18 x 13 x 8 inches
- Weight: 9.2 pounds
- Charging time: Approximately. 1-1.5 hrs
- Flight time: about 23 minutes
- Control distance: 5 km

*You can find this product on airdronesale.com with $75 discounted price for our e-book readers. Promotion code is: EBOOKPROMO (First 100 Readers)

4.2: YUNEEC Q500 4K Typhoon

Features

- 3-Axis Gimbal
- GPS positioning
- No Fly Area operate to keep FAA compliant

- 4k video
- 12MP photos
- Autonomous journey modes
- Live FPV loading to your controller

Specs
- Frequency: 2.4Ghz
- Weight: 3.7 pounds
- Charging time: Approximately. 1-1.5 hrs
- Flight time: up to 25 minutes

4.3: 3D Robotics Iris+

Features
- Autonomous journey technology
- Easily strategy flight tickets with the Droidplanner 2 app
- 16 to 22 minute journey time

Specs
- Frequency: 2.4Ghz
- Weight: 2.82 pounds
- Flight time: 16 – 22 minutes
- Control distance: 999 m

4.4: Bird AR.Drone 2.0

Features

- 360 level flips in either direction
- 720p HD camera
- Video storage on the fly with distant program or with USB display drive
- JPEG photo capture
- Charge battery energy in any USB outlet
- Flash memory: 4GB
- Easily update to meet FAA requirements

Specs

- Frequency: 5GHz
- Gyro: 3 axis
- Size: 23 x 5 x 23 inches
- Weight: 4 pounds
- Charging time: 90 minutes
- Flight time: 10-15 minutes
- Control distance: 50 meters

4.5: DJI Motivate 1 PRO

Features

- Intelligent journey modes: Follow Me, Reason for Interest, Waypoints, Course Secure, Home Lock
- One-button getting and takeoff
- Built-in 4K HD Zen use X5 movie capability
- 16-megapixel camera
- FPV digital camera ability using your cellular device
- 94-degree wide angle lens
- Flight period of up to 25 minutes
- Arms progress up and out of the camera's perspective in flight
- Gimbal rotates 360 degrees to perspective the globe around your drone

Specs

- Frequency: 2.4GHz
- Gimbal: 3-axis 360-degree spinning gimbal
- Size: 20 x 15 x 15 inches
- Weight: 6.5 pounds
- Flight time: 18 minutes
- Control distance: 2000m

CHAPTER FIVE

How To Generate Income From Drones

A couple of decades back again, drones were seen as nothing more than fancy toys for the super-rich or gimmicky monitoring devices for top-level protection and army causes. But fast-forward and a decade down the line, it has become incredibly simpler and cheaper for acquiring and get even outstanding spec UAV's that have fantastic capabilities.

The possibilities of commercializing a drone are even better and bigger, especially with the giant strides that have been produced in the over previous times 5 decades in producing impressive quadcopters as smaller sized gadgets. And if you have been looking for successful methods to create a reasonable side income from your newly acquired drone, then here's a fast primer on some of the best, easy methods of turning your drone into a cash churning program.

Current technologies have progressed to a spot that student unmanned aerial systems (SUAS), essentially activity sized distant control aircraft and choppers, are more available now than ever before, both in conditions of their relatively low expenses and simplicity of journey control for new RC aviators. Quadcopters like the DJI Phantom series seem almost ubiquitous now – they're everywhere. Cameras too, have come a long way; they are smaller sized, lighter, shoot in much higher resolutions and have better lenses. It was only a case of your energy before the two would be paired using relatively innovative, but also cost-effective, digital image stabilization gimbals developing movie and photographic aerial visuals easy, cost-effective and fun!

5.1: Survey:

Did you know that there are huge tracks of place in the world, especially in the USA and UK that are yet to be effectively mapped or demarcated? Surveyors lately started choosing drones to assist them in the applying out of boundaries and undocumented terrains on their qualities. Not only are drones cheaper than contracting satellite TV images from space, but they can fly, get in near proximity and catch more in-depth images of the swathe of place in the query than you can get from satellite TV images.

5.2: Shooting Songs Vides, TV Shows, Promotions and Mini-movies:

This is where there is a ton of cash to become. Unlike all the above ideas, which can get you just a few hundred at the most, you can create thousands by specializing on using your drone in the movie and delight market.

Both local and international artists are always looking for methods to outpace others by putting together well thought out video clips. The most recent fashion has been employing drones to movie video clips and films from very attractive and unusual perspectives. And not surprisingly, the cheques here are a bit heftier given that it easy these times to take benefit of the advertisements and video clips shot. If anything, this might be one of the few methods use your drone for the shortest efforts and still create a lot of cash in the process.

5.3: Use Your Drone Set-Up To Secure Stay Sport Matches:

This applies mainly to little league games that are yet having fun with the perks of economic live protection. It is an opportunity that is yet to be completely exploited and with a few connections, you can readily win a contract to guard a couple of live soccer, cricket or hockey suits using your drone. Of course, you will need to collaborate with a commentary on the floor for the audio, but, hey, splitting a fat cheque has never been a problem. The good thing of this is that you won't have to commit 100% of your amount of your energy in capturing the suits thus enabling you adequate of your energy and sources to project in another successful market as an additional side hustle.

5.4: Mapping:

Drones can come with some pretty clever program these times, some of which allows for accurate 3D maps to be produced from aerial movie clips. Mapping solutions are needed in the farming, mining and residence sectors, and a birds-eye perspective provides a fast and effective way of doing factors.

It's not just about a high-definition movie and imaging. LIDAR (Light Recognition and Ranging) applying instead, relies upon on a laser scanning device installed onto your drone. These technologies are can look at the height of factors on the floor below. Developed with a LIDAR scanning device, you can cover huge expenses in just a few hours, and use the details collected to develop specific digital types of landscapes. LIDAR receptors also have the bonus of being able to penetrate dense forests and vegetation, which makes it possible to scan floor that would be invisible to satellite TV or standard visuals.

5.5: Banner Advertising:

"Hey, that factor can fly. Let's fasten an email to it and parade it over many of people!" This seems to be the reasoning behind drone marketing ad campaigns and, although it's simplistic, there's certainly a sell for it. Having said that, guidelines in many nations currently forbid traveling drones over or near to crowd, so it's probably going to stay a market sector for now. But hey, that doesn't stop you from asking for your buddy a few dollars to strap "Will you marry me?" onto your drone and fly it over him having dinner with his girlfriend. Precision romance.

Companies are beginning to spring up, devoted to making marketing campaigns and promotional moments with the use of drones. This can be something as easy as traveling a marketing with an email over a meeting, to managing an aerial light display above a music concert.

5.6: Online Jobs:

Fiverr.com and other similar websites are also another option for generating an income. You can put your advertisement (gig) and you can offer your clients like: "I can prepare you a drone videography & photography" etc. as other sellers. There are not a lot of seller in this subject on Fiverr.com at the moment. And there are more other pages like Fiverr.

CHAPTER SIX
Drone photography and Videography

Inexpensive consumer drones that convenience of flights and the very best photography and videography have exploded on the market lately, developing what can only be described as drone mania among a diverse wide range of prospective clients. Because camera drones are still only available on the edge between activity and mainstream, there is a lot of confusion about what these little drones are able to do. Your choice to buy one is just the first in a lengthy flow of factors a new proprietor must think about.

Photography and videography using drones are designed to help you make use of the possibilities these nimble, cost-effective, and available traveling gadgets have created for photography and videography.

6.1: 7 Techniques for Beginning a Drone Digital Photography and Video Business

Are you a photography enthusiast? Do you engage in this leisure activity just for fun or strategy on launching an organization of your own? Well, you should be thrilled to comprehend that there are plenty of choices these times for seasoned professional photographers to begin with their profession of this type and generate profits. Although some people are born with this talent, some may study it using so many techniques on the market on YouTube and other public networking sites. Regardless of which classification you fall under, there is something that can create you think seriously about eBay and that is aerial photography. With the advent of high-tech cost-effective drones on the market, this term is now becoming more and more typical and a lot of people are already earning millions of revenues using drone photography.

If you have been of this type for a while, you're already acquainted with competitors that exist in the place of photography.

Some are devoted to the wedding or fashion photography, while others keep their choices start. They catch organic scenes, portraits, and many other kinds of images using very outstanding high-quality digital cameras. Actually, in-depth understanding of you is as essential as you, the professional photographer. If you are unknown with complete functionalities of you, you will not be able to make use of it in drone photography.

With such huge competitors, there is little room for errors if you really want to succeed. So, if you are considering of using drone photography as your profession, this content provides guidance to help you minimize threats and luxuriate in eBay as it flourishes. Here we have collected some suggestions from knowledgeable professional photographers who say that if they had known before they wouldn't have devoted these errors in the starting of their profession. So, let's go through some of these suggestions.

1. Get drone training

Flying your drone is not as easy as it might seem... at least in the beginning. There is a number of managers as well as other available choices that you need to comprehend before you can professional the expertise. If you strategy on traveling the drone yourself for catching aerial images, it is strongly advised that you first get drone coaching to make sure a secure journey and also do not into lawful problems. There are unique colleges and coaching companies now available that enroll students in their programs and when the courses are finished, they are given some kind of certification or level that reflects their command over drones or UAV traveling. You need to comprehend not just the various components of a drone but also the control buttons and sticks on the distant operator that techniques the drone and takes images. There are choices of slanting and spinning that only innovative drone aviators are able to use. Get practical the essential material and then make out the print thoroughly along with practicing every day to professional this expertise.

2. Buy the right drone

The first and most essential choice after studying is choosing the right drone for your photography & videography or different kind of business with a camera drone. You should not go and buy a drone, because it looks like good and it has a digital camera. You need to buy an effective camera drone which is able to catch quality images and loaded with the newest applications. If you have one that you are controlling with you smart phone & tablet, you should also check available applications for the best control and quality. The tools and procedures that come with a programs program help to save a lot of persistence for upcoming projects. All you need is to get a little more acquainted with the instructions and you're all set to go. Special coaching is available for some particular drone designs. Make a little research on the internet to see what other professional drone photographers are using and then try to check more details in your budget.

3. Rent a drone first

There is a choice of renting a drone to comprehend its features before actual cash on a particular design. This is a great choice for starters who have limited price range set for investing in this type of organization. There are companies that lease various types of drones and you can see their sites for more details. You have to specify a pickup time frame and revenue time frame for the drone you want to book. There is a fee associated with everyday utilization of such a leased tool and you need to take care to avoid harm, damage, and loss.

4. Set a budget

With so many amazing drones out there along with all the program and hardware they come with, you are sure to become overwhelmed. However, meticulous considering what you really need, to begin with, your own drone business allows avoiding paying for factors and gadgets you don't need. It's best to invest cash in the starting of any organization enterprise but it's also recommended not to get over excited with your investing. You must be advised that in the beginning you might experience difficulties and hurdles as it's quite typical with any other organization. Aerial photography is no different. So, set a cost-effective and keep to it especially in the first few months so that you are prepared to experience the difficulties and also be devoted to your goals.

5. Get your drone insured

While using your drone for a professional purpose, it always suggested to get it covered for potential damages that might happen. Yes, you can think that you are only flying for your business but there can be a lot of problem which you don't expect. For example; it looks funny but your drone can fall and hit somebody's car or more tragically, somebody's head. So, you should keep in mind all potential problems especially if you are planning to start with your own organization with you camera drone. Normally, these kinds of problems don't exist in the other forms of photography & videography, but flying with your camera on the air, it's different. Insurance companies have already started to make these kind of insurances, focusing your drone and its damages. You can also check it online and get a hundreds of offer.

6. Find a place to target

There are plenty of possibilities when it comes to getting aerial images but you need to concentrate on only one market or subject to concentrate on. Getting an already working as drone professional photographers in the realty organization. There is an enormous perspective of this type as new qualities, houses and apartments are always in outstanding requirement. People want to see aerial images of what they buy. Similarly, many people are choosing drone professional photographers these times to guard their unique occasions particularly weddings and engagements. Land assessing and building examination are also becoming popular in the drone market. So, before you choose, to begin with, your photography organization, it makes sense to think of a market to concentrate on so that you can concentrate your abilities on that market and gives your solutions very clearly and concisely.

7. Join the internet communities

Once you are prepared to take on your first assignment, don't forget to sign up with sites like jobfordrones.com or other public networking groups that help drone aviators discover outstanding jobs on the internet. You can discuss your sections of expertise to attract clients from around the globe and also see what other drone aviators or drone professional photographers are up to. Fiverr.com is another amazing community to generate some clients easily. It's an outstanding and free cost way of developing an impressive portfolio to become the foundation of your upcoming camera drone business.

Log on to one of the sites described above to see what other people are asking for their aerial photography solutions. To be able to develop an outstanding user profile with a number of opinions that are positive, you might need to provide your solutions at inexpensive rates in the starting. However, once you get scores, you can gradually boost your rate to generate more profits. Digital photography is an art and it should be completely enjoyed. Make sure that you polish your drone photography abilities to take your business to the next stage and get ahead of your opponents of this type.

Whenever new technologies are presented to the global world, problems and mistakes can occur. But what is important is not to repeat these mistakes later on and to comprehend from the experiences of others who tried, failed, then tried again and succeeded. Aerial photography is undoubtedly not able to eBay as more high-tech and innovative drones are being presented to the market. If you love this leisure activity and would like to convert it into a lucrative organization, do adhere to the above-mentioned suggestions to guarantee success in the lengthy time.

CHAPTER SEVEN

A Beginner's Secrets and Techniques for Learning How to Fly a Drone

Drones are the hottest topic going around the technical globe these times and everyone is trying to obtain one of them. Whether you are a wedding photographer who wants to take your business up a level or you are a hobbyist looking for some, it's essential to figure out how to fly a drone the right way. Although they are quite little in proportions it isn't easy to fly these unmanned aerial vehicles, drones. This content focuses on the key factors to know when traveling your drone.

7.1: Obstacles in Flying Drones

There are several hindrances you may experience when studying how to fly a drone. They include:

- ✓ The drone does not stay constant in air.
- ✓ The drone does not adhere to instructions.
- ✓ The drone's motions are jerky.

These are just a few of the conditions the new fliers experience when studying how to fly a drone. To obtain the hang of traveling a UAV, you must make sure that you know everything about its working principle.

7.2: Terminologies Involved in Flying Drones

You may have look at the instructions that comes with your drone but more often than not this isn't enough. You will need to comprehend a few terms if you want to figure out how to fly your drone like a professional.

There are a few typical conditions that you should know about when studying how to fly a drone. This include:

- ✓ The line of a site: This is the direct visualization of your drone while you are traveling it.

✓ FPV or first individual view: You as an airplane lead can see your drone through you.

7.3: Parts of Drones

When studying how to fly a drone, there are key sections of the drone that you need to know such as:

✓ The transmitter or distant control: This is the primary managing device that lets you fly and control the drone.

✓ Propellers: These are four in the wide range and help the drone in removing from the floor as well as maintaining a horizontally constant position.

✓ Camera: This is not existing in all the drones and is optional but allows in order to keep the lead advised about the surroundings of the drone.

✓ The frame: The structure joins all the various components and keeps them set up. The structure comes in two arrangements such as X or +

✓ The motors: There are four engines in a drone and that is why it is also known as the quadcopter. Each propeller is operated by a single engine. The voltage of the engine will figure out the rate or spinning of the propeller.

✓ Electronic rate control: The wires that connect battery energy with the engine are known as ECS.

✓ Flight control board: This is the professional control and regulates the accelerometer as well as the pyrometer directing the rate of the engine.

✓ Battery and charger: This is significant as it provides the lifestyle to the drone to take flight tickets.

7.4: Controls of the Drone

When studying how to fly a drone, it is an essential view the following controls:

✓ Roll: This is used to go the drone remaining or right usually using the right keep on the distant control

✓ Pitch: This is the slanting of drone and is done by forcing the right keep ahead or in reverse.

✓ Yaw: This is the spinning of drone in remaining or right route by shifting the remaining key towards remaining or right. This assists in changing the route of your drone.

✓ Throttle: If you want your drone to enhance or less than its existing squeeze use the remaining key to engaging and disengage it by forcing the key forwards and backward respectively.

✓ Trim: This is adjusting the aforementioned features in case you want to modify the stability of the product and can be done with the help of the control buttons on a distant program.

✓ Rudder: Controlling law is the primary operate of rudder which is also the remaining stick

✓ Aileron: Same as right stick

✓ Elevator: Same as right keep continuing to go forwards and backward.

7.5: Modes of Drone Flying

When studying how to fly a drone, you should be acquainted with the techniques in which your drone can fly. This include:

✓ Manual: you can modify all the positions of the drone manually. You need to operate it in and uneven.

✓ Auto stage or altitude: in this method, the leveling of the drone is done by itself when the keep is launched to its neutral position.

✓ GPS hold: in this method, the quadcopter will return to its original position when the keep is launched.

7.6: Mastering the Controls

When studying how to fly a drone you should professional the managers of the drone before you take on obligations outside of traveling for leisurely factors. Identical to driving, in the starting, it may appear to be an extremely tough job but as you get used to it, you will not even think before you make any shift.

The primary part to keep in a product is that you need to push the keep gently for smoother motions of the drone. You must begin by shifting the drone a little bit in each route. Knowing the managers and how they jobs are the key to traveling this revolutionary product smoothly and moreover it is the dexterity and fast response time that will help you fly your drone like a professional.

7.7: Operating the Remote Control

The distant program, which is also known as the transmitter, is the single factor that will let you eliminate the drone and fly it in the way you want it to. The name transmitter is an apt one because it transmits alerts to the drone as soon as you progress the keep or press the control buttons.

You can easily fly your drone using the keep and the key on the distant program. However, before you come up with a complete fledged journey you must first cut and modify the managers so that the drone remains instability. When for the new, you try to lift the drone using your distant program you will notice that the crone tilts one way and also moves in that route. This is one good reason you think it is hard to fly this revolutionary product initially. This happens because the stability is not right and you need to modify the content shift, yaw, and accelerator accordingly so that while raising up the drone maintains a horizontal position parallel to the floor.

In conclusion, studying how to fly a drone can be a lot of fun and can generate you some additional money, but there are processes and techniques you must be professional before you threat failing your drone, or more intense, causing bodily harm.

CHAPTER EIGHT

Uses, Safety and Legal Guidelines for Flying a Drone for Enjoyment

Everybody seems to be in love with drones these times. These traveling robots managed by a distant operator are used for fun and delight all over the globe. Designed like a quadcopter, with or without a digital camera, these gadgets look awesome and gives impressive efficiency to the consumer. However, before you effort to fly such an airplane, you need to view the suggestions carefully otherwise you might end up harming yourself or someone else. Furthermore, there are some lawful implications of this an unmanned aerial vehicles because it might place over unknown territory and infringe on somebody's personal residence.

8.1: Personal Use of Drones

The use of drones or unmanned aerial vehicles can be divided into two categories: individual and professional. Personal use indicates you want to fly such a process just for fun and do not have any aim of promoting the content you gather when you fly your drone here and there. Commercial use indicates using the details for the reason of getting money or promoting it to a third party for a benefit. In the U.S. Declarations, professional use of drones needs unique approval from the FAA. However, individual use is permitted under certain circumstances considering that the consumer follows some well-defined suggestions.

You just need to keep in mind that individual use of drones is not accompanied by many strict policies. You can fly a drone for entertainment and even take images and history video clips type of use. However, there are a few protection suggestions that have to be followed to make sure a secure and totally enjoyable experience. Moreover, you need to be advised that there are some no-fly areas everywhere in the globe and you must at all expenses avoid those locations when traveling drones.

8.2: Want to Pursue Drone Flying as a Hobby?

Here are some protection and lawful ideas for a starter to be able to have fun with this leisure activity to its fullest:

✓ Make sure that you don't take your body to an elevation more than 400 legs otherwise it might go out of perspective and become hard to manage.

✓ Your drone should stay in front of your eyes at all times.

✓ Unmanned aerial vehicles are not permitted to interfere in them of an operated airplane so be sure that you keep your body away from that type of aerial vehicles.

✓ If you think you cannot adhere to your drone everywhere, arrange for an assistant who will keep an eye on the drone at all times so that it doesn't disappear.

✓ Try to discover a place for pursuing this leisure activity where there are not many people especially youngsters.

✓ Even if you do see people around, try to keep your range and sustain it at 25 legs away to avoid accident and harm.

✓ Avoid traveling a drone when you are intoxicated or under the influence of drugs.

✓ Drones are not easy to fly especially for a novice customer who has no prior experience of traveling such a process. So, be sure you obtain adequate information to operate and how to fly it securely before you effort to fly a drone.

✓ Avoid traveling over personal residence to be able to avoid from legalities of intruding, eavesdropping and the like.

✓ If you are using a camera-fitted drone, be sure you don't photograph people without their explicit authorization. Also, avoid going to community venues where people anticipate a certain individual convenience and they don't want to see drones traveling over their heads.

It's a wise choice to comprehend on the internet for convenience plan presented by companies relevant to aeronautics and aeronautical engineering. This is to make sure that you don't infringe upon somebody's right to convenience even if it's a community residence or position. There are some locations that drones are allowed but photography is not. You'll also have certain areas where traveling a drone and catching photos both are allowed and then there are locations where drones are not permitted to enter. These are known as no-fly area. So, to be able to comprehend everything relevant to this issue, it needs to go through on the internet convenience plan.

8.3: Commercial Use of Drones

Organizations like Academy of Model Aeronautics (AMA) allow us some protection suggestions to make sure nobody gets hurt when drones are used on an industrial or individual stage. It might be of interest that you study and totally adhere to these suggestions especially if you want to use a drone for some professional use. This is to make sure that you don't experience any problem with regard to accidental injuries or harm or intrude on somebody else's residence. You should also be conscious if a certain type of organization use needs approval from the FAA.

There are companies in the US and the UK that are currently using drones for professional factors. If they have taken protection approval from the FAA, they are not doing anything unlawful. Some examples of people or companies that have been given exemptions to fly drones consist of farm owners, medical facilities, protection organizations, and railroads. The firms also have to bring up the type of airplane they will be using and the location where that airplane will be used. Most of these firms only need approval for photography, videography, and cinematography. Some other professional uses consist of aerial record applying, inspections, details acquisition and selection, search and save, sales demonstrations, crop assessing, and car accident reconstructions.

Certainly, you do not have any of the above-mentioned uses of drones when you fly such a process to keep things interesting. So, there is no need to be afraid of lawful repercussions when you are attempting to fly an unmanned aerial vehicle with the help of a distant operator without any aim of harming someone. Whether you want to fly drones just in the interest of fun or some professional use, simply be sure you obtain enough information about these little yet impressive gadgets to be able to do not into problems. Just keep under consideration the above-mentioned suggestions when you effort to fly a drone just in the interest of fun next occasion and you are all set to go!

Drones are unmanned a little bit managed traveling automobiles that also can be used for particular operate moreover to just being able to fly around. Whether bigger or small drones, a few requirements below will help you know what is best for you.

- ✓ Ease of Use (How easy is it to fly?)
- ✓ Size (The best drone overall isn't the best small drone, and the best small drone isn't the best micro drone - these matters can get actual small)
- ✓ Battery Life
- ✓ Safety (Some drones have soft external locations to avoid, say, a cracked TV screen)
- ✓ Camera (Some drones come with digital cameras, and digital cameras can be connected to most of the ones that don't)
- ✓ Value for cash (We anticipate efficiency to improve along with price)
- ✓ Features (this may the most unimportant requirements - because one would prefer a really powerful small drone with lesser features to one that can't fly well but has a lot of additional functionality)
- ✓ Other differences between drones comprise of the traveling range; 25 moments on an assortment energy cost for the Bird and up to 40 moments for the DJI Phantom. The DJI Phantom is also a little bit bulkier and some reports say that it provides better stability in windy circumstances, but both drones are reasonably constant for that. Replacement locations are readily available to buy from Amazon for both designs.

Drones have been becoming more popular and more and more professional programs allow us for them. The two primary opponents are Bird who has now launched the 2.0 version of their AR Drone for amateurs, and DJI Phantom which releases PRO drone editions.

Are you intrigued about being able to fly it around your city and take images from perspectives and perspectives you could not access before?

The fantastic information is that HD digital cameras have become cheaper and cheaper these times and both the Bird AR Drone and the DJI Phantom have them.

The updated editions come with GPS ability and a 'return home' operate designed in.

1. They can be your Wi-Fi hotspot which joins to your Smartphone or tablet and this enabling it to flow HD movie directly to your body.

2. You can also control the drone by slanting your phone ahead, backward, remaining or right, just as you would in a traveling game. The primary technological innovation in a drone consist of some type of energy plant, some propulsion procedure, some type of guiding procedure, some type of receptors to recognize position and path and a sender-receiver device to transmit and receive alerts for guiding and documenting.

3. Drones are discovered in all forms you can get in higher aircraft, and also in all type of exotic forms, like oblong airships, disks, triangles, donuts, stars or can resemble big insects or wild birds.

Safety/Regulations

Since most uses of drones are held key or simply not announced publicly, it's hard to provide a complete account of the extent of their use and who are using them but a fairly clear image emerges based on official sources, journalistic and scientific articles, advertisements from drone producers, and stories of people arriving in touch with drones in use.

Given that bigger drones are comparable to other air automobiles, they are obliged to keep lamps and another method for warning against the possibility of accident, but since govt instances working drones typically want to keep the journey key, such lamps will possibly be lit only when other visitors in the neighbourhood, or when the operators want visual contact.

CHAPTER NINE

How to Keep Your Drone Safe

Every season more people, companies, and companies are utilizing the advancements of drone technological innovation. As the number of drones is increasing, so are a number of laws and guidelines, guidelines, and suggestions to promote the best use of drones.

Businesses are using drones to expand their solutions, companies want to improve the total well being of their people (presumably), and people, usually, just want to have fun. Whatever is the reason, here are some suggestions so you can use your drone in the safest possible way.

I know how hard it can be, but once you have your drone you need to take it easy and not fly it right away. This is a new technological innovation and even if you are familiarized with drones you cannot threat neglect the just because you are too lazy to view the instructions. It will take you only a couple of moments to comprehend at least what you consider an essential location so you can be sure that you know how to operate it.

9.1: Laws and regulations:

Another critical facet is to obey the guidelines of the concentrate which you intend to fly your drone. They differ based on where you are, but usually, they are very much as well. Most of the guidelines talk about how outstanding your drone can go. The FAA stipulates that a drone cannot improve than 120m (400 feet).

A different limitation to traveling your drone is not how outstanding but where you can take it. There are certain locations where it is forbidden to fly a drone. An example is within 5 miles of an airport. You cannot fly a drone over people or automobiles because this could be looked at as a threat for both and you will be accountable for any harm caused for your drone. The good way is to get advised about the guidelines and the areas where the drone is to be used.

9.2: Do not reduce sight:

Another essential protection guidance (and a law as a case of fact) is that you fly your drone only as far as you can see it and no further than that. I don't think that I should even explain this, but just to be sure here it goes: Leaving your drone can be really dangerous for those on the floor as well as costly should you reduce your drone completely. If you cannot see your drone there's a chance you can reduce communication with the operator and reduce finish control. Although many drones have 'return to safety' ability which allows them to send returning to their spot to start, it is still advised not to project so far so that you forget your drone.

9.3: When to fly:

Checking the climate can help figure out when's an outstanding or a bad a chance to fly them. Although some drones display no problems to fly on gloomy times, others do display some deficiencies under these circumstances. Again, reading the information makes sense.

In the case when you not only have gloomy times but also powerful gusts of the wind, no issue how outstanding your drone is, it is a bad concept to fly them. The gusts of wind could make it harder to maneuver the drone and it can go anywhere. Again, it is not important how outstanding your drone is, if it could eventually actual dimension choppers, it will eventually your drone too. On times with powerful gusts of wind, keep your drone at your house.

9.4: Check components:

So now that you have look at the information and got all the details you need to fly your drone, you are prepared to have some fun with it, right? Well, not quite. Although you know the theory, you still have to evaluate that the drone is functioning effectively. You need to evaluate that every component is in top condition. This includes propellers, battery energy, lights and everything connected to the drone. And this has to be done every single time you are traveling the drone. Whenever that the drone is going to be used it needs to be checked.

9.5: Use apps:

A lot of companies offer an app for smartphones that help aviators control their drones. If you have it, then it is very likely that the app has a choice to help you calibrate your drone. This is a useful gizmo to make sure that various components are working correctly and you can go traveling your drone without any worries.

9.6: Get permission:

Finally, if your drone has a digital camera and is able to take images or video clips, then you need to have authorization from the proper regulators to take an image or video clips clip, otherwise, it is unlawful to do so.

So here you go, you have a starter list of factors to take into consideration before traveling your drone. Many guidelines described are actually laws and guidelines to guard people around you and even yourself and they differ based on where you are. Others are just for your own outstanding. All in all, they are intended to help to create your experience of drone traveling an outstanding high-quality one.

CHAPTER TEN
REGULATION OF DRONES

The increased use of drones for private programs has presented many nations with regulatory difficulties. Such difficulties consist of the need to make sure that drones are operated securely, without harming the community and nationwide protection, and in a way that would protect sections of nationwide, historical, or organic significance. A wide range of the nations surveyed in this report has also created efforts to address concerns regarding the residence and convenience privileges of landowners or other people impacted by the operating of drones.

You obtained drone. And you're probably chomping at the bit to get battery energy charged and take it out for the first test journey. But before you do, you need to know about the policies that the Government Aircraft Management (FAA) has set up for traveling drones in the U.S and UK And you should also know about your privileges and the privileges of those around you.

10.1: Registration

The very first factor a new drone proprietor needs to do is to sign-up it with the federal govt. If that sound a bit Big Brotherish, it is. But after a swath of crashes and violations of the common guidelines of the air that were trumpeted on the nightly information and blogosphere, the FAA instituted the signing up program.

Registration expenses $5, but you can avoid that fee if you sign-up before Jan. 21, 2016. There is a grace period, but if you're caught traveling a drone that's unregistered, municipal penalties of up to $27,500 may be evaluated (although you'll have until Feb. 19 before they can be assessed).

We are in the age of constant discovering of new technological innovation and the globe seems not to be prepared to relax yet. Humans all over the globe are regularly and passionately interesting in one discovering or the other. The whole essence of this research is aimed at ensuring a lifestyle of convenience and convenience. It is this quest for convenience that led them to the innovation of drones.

Drones with their advantages also have many drawbacks. They can be used to spy on an innocent. It can lead to invasion of convenience. Since drones are too easy to buy now, it becomes a serious concern. Almost anyone can go into an electronics shop and buy a drone off the shelf for only $ 100. And if it lands in the wrong arms, several problems can arise. To mitigate this, several nations are coming up with their own laws and guidelines so as to safeguard their people. A while ago, an 11-year-old girl was hit with the debris of a failing drone. Moreover, aviators have reported almost two dozen near misses with drones. Maintaining these problems under consideration, it is extremely necessary that laws and guidelines on drones become and even more necessary that the most popular man knows about these laws and guidelines.

We would, for the time-being, be discussing the laws and guidelines in the United States of America.

10.1: UNITED STATES OF AMERICA:

In United States of America, there are laws and guidelines that are managing the use or implementation of your drone. Let us have a look at some of the laws and guidelines.

1. REGISTRATION OF DRONES WITH THE FEDERAL AVIATION AUTHORITY (FAA):

It is the plan of this statutory body, whose duties are to regulate actions in the USA airspace, that any drone that weighs more than 55lbs or less than that must be authorized by the FAA. Not only this signing up is limited to Americans and lawful permanent residents. The reasoning of this signing up is to avoid violation of other people convenience.

2. COMMERCIAL USE OF DRONES:

The laws and guidelines managing the use of drones in the USA, do not allow you to fly your drones without acquiring a particular approvals that let you fly professionally while you are getting a benefit. If the drone is not to be used for professional and commercial reasons, it is not necessary to get approved.

3. PERSONAL USE:

There is no law on the individual use of drones other than the law that is presently managing the use of design airplane. However, while using the drone type of use, there are some limitations that it cannot be traveled in locations known as "NO FLY ZONES". These consist of the White House, the nature and any other essential installation of the country.

4. GUIDELINES FOR FLYING:

You are to keep the journey of your drone within the elevation restricts of 400 legs. You are to keep your individual drones within eyesight and possibly with the employment of a professional if there is the need for that. You are also unlikely to intentionally fly over unprotected people, insecure qualities, and shifting automobiles. Above all, you are to keep a range of 25 legs from insecure people.

5. SURVEILLANCE:

You are not to conduct monitoring actions with your drone in a place wherever convenience is needed without express authorization.

6. IMPLICATION OF NOT REGISTERING:

The law makes it compulsory that you are to sign-up your drone. Failure to do so will be tantamount to criminal acts and the penalty is an excellent of $250,000 or 36 months imprisonment.

10.2: UNITED KINGDOM

It will interest readers to know that a 42-year-old man was convicted in the U.S. on September 16, 2015, for traveling a drone without acquiring authorization. His drone was traveled over a stadium. According to the Metropolitan Police, this was the first conviction in respect of unlawful drone traveling. This is to tell us about the severity of not acquiring authorization before traveling drones. It also tells us that the drones are no longer in use by the army only. They are implemented for various factors such as search and save operations, distribution of hospital devices to distant and inaccessible locations. Farmers also are engaged in the use of this excellent innovation of technological innovation for aerial monitoring of their farm generate. What an outstanding innovation indeed.

Talking of laws and guidelines relating to drones in the USA, the company that is accountable with the control over the airspace is the Civil Aircraft Power (CAA). There are some policies which must be totally checked before setting up your drones in the USA.

1. COMPULSORY REGISTRATION:

The House of Lords (EU Committee) has necessary the compulsory signing up for both personal and professional utilization of drones in the UK. This call came as a result of fear that many people do not have the adequate understanding of aviation guidelines.

2. RESTRICTED FLYING ZONES:

At existing in the UK, there are no particular guidelines or guidelines that prohibit the buy of drones, but there are restrictions on the bodyweight and traveling areas. Your drones must weigh less than 20 KGs and must not be used for professional factors. Also traveling is limited to 150 meters within a congested place.

3. FLIGHT WITHIN SIGHT:

Drones journey must be within perspective. This signifies that you cannot go beyond the controlled restrict of 400 legs in elevation while flying. Maximally, CAA allows you to fly 500 legs horizontally. Should there be the need for your drone to go beyond these controlled limits, you are to file a program to the company seeking its approval first.

4. COMMERCIAL USAGE:

The Civil Aircraft Power (CAA) also makes it compulsory that professional utilization of drones needs to be authorized by the company. In issuing a license, the applicant must display a good evidence of competence and experience in the use of drones.

There is no doubt about the proven reality that drone technologies have indeed created lifestyle simpler than ever before in many factors. However, with entertainment come obligations. No one has the ability to infringe upon the privileges of others under the pretext of delight and convenience. Maintaining this under consideration, the aviation regulators have come up with the aforementioned laws and guidelines. Regardless of how harsh they seem, they are for the best of people. We hope that clients would totally adhere to the guidelines set down by their specific nations to avoid any dangerous incident.

CHAPTER ELEVEN

Drones and Weather

In previous times, drones were used primarily for army and monitoring factors, but there have been several technologies in their style and implementation over the decades. Nowadays, drones are used in several different locations. They are used in gathering details for research factors, visitors control, aerial photography, farming, movie production, information protection and so many others. They are now also being used in the preparing and predicting of climate. This content examines different methods that climate drones can be implemented and how it could help forestall the loss of lives and qualities through early detection techniques.

Climate change and the resultant disruptions to varying weather conditions globally is a major challenge and there is no better here we are at climate drones, which will be used for the reason of research, research, and evaluation of these changes.

Drones are already being used in various research works which help predict varying weather conditions accurately. Veerabhadran Ramanathan, a researcher at the Scripps Institute of Oceanography had previously conducted researches using bigger airplane but discovered that it was a very costly project. He later realized that it would be cheaper and simpler to use drones for the same objective at a much more cost-effective. In the course of his execute, he flew three drones.

(Drones) over the Indian Ocean from where he and his group collected details which showed that black carbon was the second largest cause of climatic change.

They are also being used to gather details which will help to make predictions and documenting climate styles. There is really no gainsaying that drones will play a big part in climate research in typical. Charles Mondello, a drone professional said and I quote "the drone clearly has a value add."

Lots of govt emergencies and climate control organizations over previous times several decades have been interesting in drones. Only lately, a group of scientists in Huntsville, Alabama are said to be intending to set up drones to assist them in getting outstanding high quality as well as regularity details of heat range to allow them to assess the factors in which stormy weather generate tornadoes. Also, it is worth noting that since drones operate between the earth's surface and satellite TV, scientists are excited at the prospects of using them to obtain relevant details about stormy weather and climate styles.

Drones are useful and would play a vital part in climate research. The President of the Centre for Severe Weather Research, Joshua Wurman sees drones as the next growing trend, one that could offer very valuable details for climate research.

In 2015, Oklahoma State University and several other universities entered a research partnership with a $6 million grant from National Science Foundation to allow them style and develop a drone which will help enhance climate predicting. How is this predicted to work? Drones would be implemented into other locations that have been hard to reach and very distant locations details they gather will be incorporated into climate prediction designs. The details collected will be used in preparing for upcoming years. The drones will be thought to send out details which will help evaluate the wind, thermodynamic and atmospheric chemistry parameters.

Researchers in Colorado and Nebraska have successfully implemented drones into about 10 stormy weather which included 6 extremely stormy weather and a lot of details were collected on heat range and moisture details.

There is another place which drones are to be implemented in the USA and this is known as climate modification or adjustment. Tests are being created by an organization of meteorologists in Nevada to use drones to scatter particulates of silver iodide into the reasoning program to trigger the release of rainfall or snow. This would be of big benefit to curbing drought problems which farm owners have familiar with recent times. Meteorologist Jeff Tilly has also developed such like known as a reasoning seeding rainfall generator which is to be connected to the drones during the research. These inventions are revolutionary.

CHAPTER TWELVE
Tips for Buying Your Drone

Businesses and consumers as well are discovering new purposes of drone every day. From residence to occasion photography to sports, drones are being used for a number of factors. On top of that, people are discovering drones to be an outstanding overdue activity too. This is the reason why there has been a spike in the requirement of the drones and people all over the globe are looking to buy one. However, purchasing a drone isn't simple. There are a number of factors that you need to keep under consideration before you go into the market to buy one. The following are some suggestions that are going to help you in purchasing a drone that is fit for your needs. The following locations should be examined prior to purchasing a drone.

11.1: Purpose of Use

The first tip for purchasing a drone is to identify the reason for which you want this automobile. For example, if you are looking to get this revolutionary product for purely leisurely factors then even a little, inexpensive quadcopter would be enough. However, if you want to buy the drone for professional aerial photography and videography then you will have to go for a more innovative design that is capable of doing catching images at different perspectives. For cargo holding requirements, you will need a drone that is capable of doing raising large loads and holding them over long-distance. If you intend to buy the drone for examination factors then it would be best for you to opt for a drone that can operate in unfavorable circumstances. Drones used for wildlife photography are usually very costly and should only come if you are a wildlife professional photographer who wants to catch the wildlife in their organic habitat without risking yourself.

11.2. Machinery:

Another of the part that needs to be looked at when it comes to purchasing drones is that of its devices. There are different kinds of drones available in the market but they have their own specific techniques. You have to comprehend that not all drones have the devices available to execute the features that you want them to do. For example, if you want to get the drone simply for the fun then a quadcopter with easy devices would be just excellent. However, if you strategy on using the drone for an industrial objective then the quadcopter would not be enough. You will then have to go for a drone whose devices is able enough to finish the task be it photography or package delivery.

11.3: Design:

Another tip that may be necessary sometimes when you are purchasing a drone is to have a near look at its style. Generally, all the UAVs have the same primary idea; they fly without the need of an on-board human lead. However, they differ on the foundation of their style. For example, the quadcopter has four engines to propel it and look almost like a helicopter while the army quality drones are jet fueled and look more or less the same as usual aircraft. So, unless you are in the army and are in need of a stealth drone, it would be best for you to go for a drone that has an easy style.

11.4: Camera and Gimbal Supports:

Drones are mostly being used for the reason of photography and videography. If you want to use yours for the same objective then you will need to discover one that has a digital camera installed on it. However, an ordinary digital camera won't do the job. You would need to make sure that you installed on the drone you are purchasing is a great one that can take the very best images of convenience. Another tip to keep in a product is to buy a drone that has a gimbal assistance. The gimbal assistance is going to keep you constant during the drone's journey, enabling it to take better pics and vids.

11.5: Battery Time

Battery timing is of significance too when it comes to purchasing UAVs. Generally, a quadcopter or drone will fly for around 5 to Quarter of an hour at a stretch. With a bigger battery energy, the drone usually stay airborne for more than an hour. So, it is best that you go for a drone that has an effective battery energy especially if you want to use it for aerial photography or examination factors. Make sure that battery energy the drone is rechargeable and can be easily operated up.

11.6: Range

The wide range of most of the drones is not more than 50 meters. This is usually a suitable range for getting aerial photos. However, there are innovative drones available too that have a much higher wide range. If you want the drone for wildlife photography, then it is best that you go for one that can provide you with the wide range near to 100 meters or more.

11.7: Spare Parts

Always ask the dealer to provide spares for your drone. Most of the drones available in the market come with additional rotors as these sections of the drone are fragile and can breakdown if consistently used.

11.8: Cost

The expense of the drones is dependent on their type. If you want to buy the simplest design then you won't have to invest a lot of cash on them. Still, it would be a considerable financial commitment as these drones don't come inexpensively. You can get drones cheaper online if you look for them on the internet. There are many sites offering discounts on the selling of drones and quadcopters.

In closing, there are a number of factors that you need to keep under consideration before you go into the market to buy the drone. If you take these considerations in actually will get the most out of neglect the.

CHAPTER THIRTEEN

Where to buy drones?

There are most satisfactory details on drones for selling such as scores to help create your thoughts up simpler. Buy the Best Drone provides our honest, unbiased opinions to help and create the best choice possible with your buy. We realize that purchasing a drone can be confusing for starters, so let us do the legwork while you relax and see what we're considering. This content is written with you in mind, to help your drone purchasing experience and make it easier. Keep in mind that there are a lot of type of drones such as racing-speed drones, camera drones, monitoring drones, individual drones, toy drones and army drones... Don't panic, we're here to help about drones.

Feel totally able to evaluate out drone buyer's information that covers everything from the basics for brand spanking new people to innovative drone photography suggestions to help you get the most out of the best drones. We also get drone sources offering details about the range of drones. If you're looking for a GoPro drone, look at an extensive explanation of what to look for. If you're a little enterprise, examine out our professional drones information.

Remember, traveling drones is our factor. We love them, we obsess over them, and we know them. If you're here, we're hoping you're at least enthusiastic about our passion. If you are purchasing a drone you must sign-up it with the federal govt aviation administration (FAA).

Below are some of the top shops and top drones for every expertise level:

✓ **Airdronesale.com:**

Airdronesale.com is one of the wholesale shop regarding Drones. You can find all kind of drones, parts and accessories in this online shop. They are also supported us while we are publishing our ebook.

✓ **Amazon.com:**

I do not think Amazon needs any kind of introduction. We all know we can buy anything from Amazon. Amazon is even focusing on developing its very much own drone which would deliver offers to clients in less than a half-hour.

✓ **Hobbyking.com:**

HobbyKing.com is one of the biggest shops for purchasing drones. It is often said to be the Walmart of stereo control. The products on Hobbyking are those that are manufactured by them while some are created by them while the remaining are just being sold by them. The high organization's drones on this shop vary from the best to the worst so be aware when choosing the drones. Do look at the opinions to get a better understanding of what the drone's high quality is.

✓ **RCGroups.com:**

Drones can also be discovered from the categorized section of RCGroups.com. It is thought to be the Craigslist of stereo control things. Here you would discover great offers but beware you can also be scammed. About ninety-five percent of people promoting there are perfect while the remaining five percent can be financially dangerous for you. So, take care of the remaining 5% and you will do well.

DJI:

DJI is the leader and the frontrunner in private drone market. It is a Chinese organization founded a decade before. It manufactures drones for professional as well as leisurely use. Although headquartered in China, it is spread to United States, Japan and Europe. It has higher than three thousand employees and its revenue amounted to a billion dollars.

Listed below are some of the other sites from where drones can come. The detailed sites are the top level sites as far as drone purchasing is concerned. They have had an outstanding and powerful reputation of promoting drones.

✓ **Xheli.com:**

Xheli.com is a United States based organization with headquarters in Los Angeles. It claims to have cost-effective drones for starters as well as knowledgeable ones. It has quite a number of drones which are delivered to every globe. They have a 25.000 square feet warehouse where the drones and other things are housed prepared to be shipped anywhere and to any globe.

www.ingramcontent.com/pod-product-compliance
Lightning Source LLC
Chambersburg PA
CBHW062117220526
45471CB00010B/3769